Coming Full Circle

Coming Full Circle

RKR

Copyright © 2011 by RKR.

ISBN: Softcover   978-1-4628-5241-3
           Ebook   978-1-4628-5242-0

All rights reserved. No part of this book may be reproduced or transmitted in any form or by any means, electronic or mechanical, including photocopying, recording, or by any information storage and retrieval system, without permission in writing from the copyright owner.

This book was printed in the United States of America.

To order additional copies of this book, contact:
Xlibris Corporation
1-888-795-4274
www.Xlibris.com
Orders@Xlibris.com
97113

Contents

Spring Cleaning 7
Summer Place 8
Summer Life 9
Summer Seascape 10
Defying Gravity 11
Thinking of you 12
Telophase I 13
Brief Encounters 15
Curtains Up 16
So Much Worse 18
You Come First 22
Whip it! 23
You Know Who You Are 24
Superhuman 26
Detritus 27
Signaling Dissent 28
Cheers Felisa! 29
Earning My Stripes 31
Leaf Fall 32
Autumnal Lament—Asian Style 33
Two Ways Of Looking At It 34
Garage Sale 35
Who Do You Think You Are? Some Kind Of Super Star? 36
Endeavor 38
Hidden Hungers 40
Proclamations! 41
Gladiator 42
Pep Talk 43
Separation 44
Willow Pattern—Take I 46
Willow Pattern—Take II 47
Hold The Earth 48

Spring Cleaning

Clearing her room, taking out the old, rolling in the new,
When you sell items, you won't get them back . . .
Green musical caterpillar, doggy on wheels, art works drenched in paint
Replete with dendritic cracks,
Traceable with the very tip of my index finger;
She sticks post-its on everything, $1, $5, $50 . . .
Moving speedily, a Tasmanian devil!
My whirling dervish!
With stiff upper lip, more formal, reserved and reminiscent
Of a time slightly past, they label her 'spirited'!
Indeed.
Barreling on, layering energy, open the doors, set up sale signs,
The day promises length! Anticipating the clean up, festive fingers,
Looking up from under weighty, colossus lashes,
Expectation of gusts of air as she blinks, head flinches, eyes dart,
Big brown eyes twinkle . . .
Glee . . .
An innate gleam, she's born with it, *Gaga* would relate.
Such mischievousness, cold fusion energy burning brightly blue
In such a small, six-year-old package!
Now rolling out, saved grocery ties, contemplating its placement
Amidst other highly valuable possessions, brushing back a single tuft of hair,
Hair bands are not sweatbands, I explain, she hops past me.
Like Luke with the force, it's a sense:
A kangaroo in her past life,
Speaking to the ether, following her out,
Wondering what will she be like . . .
But I can wait, can't ask for a more perfect moment . . .
Bounding back, mommy gets a squeezy hug, a post-it on my shirt marked $20.

Summer Place

This is my place,
Summer sizzling place;
Black top stove top poaching sunny side eggs,
A queer smallish place,
With mosquito thoughts buzzing round,
In cahoots with rickety chair and bumpy bed bound
Midst wispy curtains torn and faded pink,
Cradling creaking door and cracked sink.
One window askew, it can't be budged;
The other, so sealed it's forever shut.

Paint is peeling,
Heat waves blazing,
Brown haloes on everything;
Cats are mewling even at play,
When grey mixes with night and day.

This queer hellish hot place-
Here I have the casual verve
Like Penelope to weave and unweave;
To begin each day with a sigh
And slick the salt drop from my eye
I laugh with the lone sunflower
Laughing in my backyard bower-

A weird sort of place, though
There is room and view enough
To be happy in;
To be.

Summer Life

Adobe walls painted egg white with
Green lattice of wandering vine leaves-
Blue-green algal blend of plopping crystal water from
Squat, black benign stone Neptune;
Spanish wrought iron holders clinging like
Old wives to Indian clay flowerpots;
Last lilacs laughing, caressing their Italian lanai,
Occasionally stealing out, dancing with Dutch tulips and mossy English ferns,
Bossy Malayan Acacia tree chirruping bird song to
The coy bridal greenery of native Kasoy and Kalachuchi;
A clear blessed caul of a Mediterranean sky
And a Maltese sun pouring red gold benediction down on
Dense, burnished platters laden with latest French Cordon Bleu
To tempt anew any faded, jaded Egyptian pasha . . .

I remember with rained-on face,
I remember summer life as a celebration
With fruit and wine and song
In glowing technicolor throng . . .
Summer life, all year round, light, iridescent . . .
I remember summer with my mid-winter mind . . .
Remembering grows into a habit of happiness.

Summer Seascape

Golden skins stretched in bikinis and bare bottoms,
Halo-halo vendors and bulging buco scalpers;
Racuous cries of sea gulls and land urchins
Swooping down upon silver splashed waves,
Life waves webbed in pulsing, plush fish nets,
Flotsam and jetsam of other lives, other shores
Rounded pebble smooth, shell clear, clean worn gold . . .
Through white crumpled bits of paper clouds,
Against an azure backdrop blazes this summer sun,
Showering vermilion benediction, at high noon mass,
On eyes of snails, crab tails, eel skin shards,
Purple ooze, ground gravel, crotchety corals,
Strange smelly seaweed, pinkish wimpy limpets,
Starfish and stingray and ballooning puffer fish
All speak of this blessing, this conformation,
This conflagration! The keen knife sheen of living!

Defying Gravity

(For Nancy Mairs who loves cacti, reptiles and poets—not necessarily in that order)

In this slithering snake year, life rippling into puzzling circles,
End to end in complex constellations, nerve tipping Chinese acrobatics,
I rub chafing scales to cast off my time-mottled skin,
In recurring rituals, year after year, sunk in old stone deep gloom.

You, stand stout hearted, cypress sinews, your emerald lights
Glinting green and honey in a crown of gladdening shoots,
Top seared with lightning, assailed impervious indestructible light pulsing,
I, splintered heart, scum scattered in mallard water,
Burrow deep to meet your wave on a winging incantation,
The rare magic, the right pliancy to hold sundered selves
Together. Deep in the rich loam, my searching scales
Entwine your hidden water roots. Drinking long and deep,
Not minding whiplash storms, electric bolts and sudden crust breaks,
I dream, small creature sun seeking, blue skywards,
Defying the bare gravity of stone suffering,
I dream of breaking surface into other worlds,
Other possibilities.

Thinking of you
(For Toril Moi)

I remember the light, the line, the smile,
The taut blue of the fjord in your eyes,
Crackling thunderbolts to distance my hells.
Sun kissed, mane tossed, we sipped twilight tea
(Made extra-strong I remember)
Under ink spilt skies with the hint of a tint beneath.

In constellated breaths we poked fun at Frenchmen, fads
And other figs that don't matter; by and by
We delved deep, so deep that I choked hard
In the sinking stone gloom, ribs raked under
Somber nightmares, leeches, worms and wimps;
Then your sudden sprout of interactive peacock tinged wings
That bore me in upward song, crashing, crashing
Through cascading walls of world fear!

Snug under super wings, I wondered how you
Rushed, light-speed to lode my light need
To see the world lit with meteors.
Precise pearl molting to clasp the thorn within,
Valhalla, you showed me, is here, is here
In our shared blood.

Telophase I

Just before
The finale,
The inception,
I feel I should point out—we are much more . . .
Just before the split,
The symmetry is perfect.
All that intracellular ooze
Should lay bare for all to enjoy.
Schadenfreude!

Endless permutations and combinations
And yet no one can see,
Wading through our murky cytoplasm
Without a nano-drop of waste,
Déjà-vu, a constant rhetoric of salvaging
We are so much more!
Triage? Humpty-dumpty,
And no one can fathom we are anything but more,
The emotions of randomness . . .

Scrambled eggs,
Blind, writhing wrist flinging darts through multi-dimensional space.
And let's not overlook the severe analyses . . .
Fluorescent under scrutiny, straining from the weight of giant oculars
And a thousand points of light bearing down
There *is* more here . . .
We are stained with the dye, yes, taint of existence,
Stretching like rubber bands, taught-compact DNA, dense spirals packeted
Into a microscopic sardine can

Is this what there is?
One un-unique experience of a mackerel?
Peel through the onion, diaphanous skin, pale and luminous
Perhaps with compound eyes, blink and
Vision remains clear
The private, personal spaces, our psychological labyrinth
Floating aimless yet caught in a viscous gel that adheres and self perpetuates
This is what there is . . .

Fifty percent is teetering on the edge of the precipice,
Almost through the sieve
Release the pincers, slide out the jagged fragment of glass,
There is much more
To us
Than meets the eye.

Brief Encounters
(For my mother and her mother)

"Someday soon", you said, "We'll meet again",
Disoriented by hospital space and drugged light,
Your closed blue threaded lids didn't close
Out the synchronous flight of love and life, life,
Even as the grains stood grumbling between ascent and descent;

"Someday soon!" spoke your fingers twisting into tangled skeins,
Hands trembling, remembering the weight of blue jars, blue mottled veins,
Clumps full of hair coming away with clumsy touches, whispers,
Leaving bare the top where our days, our lives were pegged.
No one noticed us, two autumn tinged leaves,
Floating away on a flimsy strand of doom.

Someday soon you'd become me, be me,
Breaking surface out of murky revisions,
Unweaving knotted tensions in alien space,
Unlocking primal prisms in the quietest of river channels,
In the quietest of mind channels;
Then we'll know our gossamer days, our moth wing lives,
Are hanging on to brief encounters, chance happenings . . .

Curtains Up

A rhythmic reverberation begins as a sixth sense,
Resounding drum-roll please
Deep voice deep throat, guttural,
Yet light-footed,
Piercing but soft,
In the recesses of the final frontier
Tentatively steps out, right foot first, pointed toe,
Wailing, the sound deepens
Pervading the matrix
Eyes open,
Realization is undeniable yet methodical.

Acknowledging the allegorical depth
Through a cochlea of memories;
How clever! Seeping in
Before sufficient spread surrenders,
Top-off the nautilus chambers; ram in a second connective siphuncle!
Spaces are filled; voices almost speak "we are legion",
Eerily familiar,
One index finger raised subconsciously, dangling in mid air,
Trying to pin it, pin the donkey, feeling pumped!
It's rare these dissolute days dissolving, rejoice, while it lasts!
Humming, buzzing, the grappling-throwing dummy doesn't stand a chance!
Not today.

Mood dresser, mood-live-er,
Imbued with sympathy, empathy, hearing you, channeling you
Symbiont, personal millennia of reincarnated personas.

Lips spread thin, just infinitesimally
Reflexive in pattern, from knowledge already known,
Some like we, like me, after all
Believe
First there was sound.
Sound before light . . .
Within ancient memory of imagination
Spirals of mist and smoke, cosmic creation, 'big bang',
Then sound, strong but ethereal, ohm-
Omnipresent,
Filling dark star-less crevices, black holes,
Named for this universe, my first child, engulfing rhythm,
Sonorous, mellowing slathered samba breezes,
Determined fingers continue digging my garden for my roots.

So Much Worse

"But my lonely is mine. Now your lonely is somebody else's. Made by somebody else and handed to you. Ain't that something? A second hand lonely."
                                        -Sula. Toni Morrison.

Sharks should have a whole week dedicated to you . . .
Why not be less like me and more like you?
Remember when? Twenty-three years of it?
Calling your name, the soft sweep of a hand on the shoulder,
180-degree fashion model turn to stun,
Stepping back, stammering apologies
Discovering I was not you—your own sibling . . .
So? Waking into facing habitual gloom,
Two years ago, one random Tuesday,
Deciding you just weren't feelin' it,
A no speak zone, you decreed,
Negating all histories of sharing, a sepulchral silence,
That's it; you're all set.

Still young, relatively,
Still haven't filled the present nor filed my history folder
It was us—you and I together, you see,
Twenty-three years, three-fourths of me and mine and thee-
Shared experience, bearing witness,
No desire to wait around,
Been there, done that?
To glimpse how it all might turn out?

Coming Full Circle

Dissolution of shared consciousness,
Inevitable aging, changing, unraveling the tangled web you wove,
Stabbing, flesh tearing, ripping like sodden cardstock,
A fire burning in my veins,
Easy to kindle but effort to keep,
Unsteadying the fevered mottling, the clotting,
I signed the maintenance contract, you?
Fingers crossed behind back?

Made you laugh when you were in despair, changed the oil, carried you . . .
G6 speeding yet steadily coveting special significance, our creed,
Before cell phones, before Internet,
Making it work, patching as we went,
Never promising easy, you acted as though you knew that.
Waking up one random Tuesday, deciding to change tires,
Wouldn't a rotation have been sufficient?

OK, you said, *you're all set*,
Finding myself blankly still standing before your
Cash and carry counter, dilemma: Paper or plastic?
Within the mire of faces, places, names, people,
Finding no signs of me,
Labeling me a particular name,
You don't get me, can't accept it,
Too weird for you,
Borderline paranormal?
Cavalier about timing, uncompassionate, unmoved,
Seeking the white hot sun, a searing urge to scorch–
Couldn't wait!
I am not you.
Cannot be you.

Bar meetings, couples double dates,
All night dancing, whooping, hollering, discussing past relationships,
Fruity concoctions in fluorescent colors, food for insipid sprawl,
Like Soutin's *Piece Of Beef*,
Straight up shots and lots of merlot moments, aid and abetting;
Later, spilling, dripping myriads of sluggish, slurring petty grievances, jealousies,
Pouring out our Boston beans.
An unholy, unseasonal *Festivus* without pole!
Laughing, crying, picking at our dates . . . double couples best friends too!
How sweet! Rolling my corneas in their hot pockets, you've seen it I do it best!
No, no, not that French ma cherie,
I'm not unidimensional; I'm no cheese chomping surrender monkey.

Working not to irritate, apologizing for being late, for being,
Choosing your orbit, blinding faith in hazy oracle prowess,
Always glad,
Empathic, channeling your moods,
Your sorrow,
Persisting to deliver cheer,
Striding forth, outstretched fingers of *Adam*,
Through clouds, perpetually reaching,
Misunderstood,
Blame for the apple! Call me *Eve*.

A foreshadowing, impending shipwreck,
Callousness, cavalier ejection, instability,
Surficial temperatures, pressures, crack the buffer,
Rip off the band-aid!
Voted off Eden, an open shaft extending to Dante's seventh layer,
Salty-iron flavored, rust encrusted remains of the day, loose ends,
And what of the apple . . .
Such waste, piteous Somalis still starving . . .

Coming Full Circle

Half chewed and spit out, boyfriend break-ups, husbands coming and going,
Counting on you to get through the through,
Ironically, a self-inflicted burden for your Atlas arms,
A Tumulus of your unyielding spirit,
Cast-off the albatross!
No more thousand-pound gorillas in the room!
Is that it?

Whirring within, jigging mind's breath,
You were my *Sula*, my *Meridian* marker . . .
That *is* it.
Toni Morrison would agree,
We were girls together,
Plague, pestilence, pox,
What you did was so much worse!

You Come First

My first time, fingers wringing, stacks of nerves,
At two weeks overdue, waiting with Becket for Godot,
I wrapped my finger impatiently,
And still at first sight you took my breath away.
You looked at me for the first time, wide-eyed,
Wise, as if you had known me,
From before . . .
You smiled a smile just for me; another first,
Not shared with anyone else, made me cry.
Everything is always new, will be new,
When it comes to you.
You raised me first and then I, you
Or was it the other way around?
Down is up for me and you. It is all a big deal
Zero experience; stubbing toes, skinning knees,
It's a scary world to take off training wheels,
When I let you out that will also be a first . . .
But please don't get too far away,
I won't stop you but you will take the first piece
Of my heart with you, you know it too.
I don't need anyone for the first clue-in that
I love you. It doesn't matter to me
What you don't do.
You will always be
My first child . . .

Whip it!

Speak to your doctor,
Start from the beginning.
Precise fingers, meticulous with purpose,
Intertwined with mine,
Brushing back a strand of hair from my eyes,
Another exact, fluid motion,
No hesitation, zero clumsiness,
We are adults!

No room here for playfulness;
Puppy love is for others-
Morons making widgets,
Let us get down to business.
Don't tremble for your beloved,
It is unnecessary, pointless,

How shiny you are!
Parched and black-topped
A suburban driveway,
My gifts dive off you,
Eggs off of *Calphalon*-
A whack from the back of the pan, in mid air,
Flung from your verbal slingshot,
The whites bounce
Off the wall,
Due to lack of binding moisture and the yolks,
They explode with sputtering sound!
Out of thought, out of dreams one by one,
Round and round I go
A roller-derby!
I exist, but
Forget to live.

You Know Who You Are

Physiological blur,
Yeats' gyres really can swirl!
Claiming confusion seems too simple,
Ease of immaturity,
A child with her blanket,
I know,
Too many reasons to choose from,
Distill down one,
Knowing me best,
Must have been impenetrable, alien metal
Needles of black basalt, searing,
Breaking skin underfoot,
Tread on! Compelled, just barely cooling,
Bubbles bursting, morphing igneous lava popping,
Open pores
Running the extent, my circular involution,
Head to foot in 3-D.

Loving the challenge or injury,
Wondering which or if at all,
Regrets only please,
Lonely is having memories and no one to share,
Manifesting guiltily, every second, every day,
Lingering, a deep-freeze,
Stratigraphic layered ice, flowing frozen robes
Blanketing this mutilated Earth,
Ever so briefly, barely, an almost imperceptible heat
Radiates beneath brittle pocked surfaces,
Beyond the mason-jar seal,
King Tut's Golden Shrines,
How did it feel to warm hands?

Should have let it be . . .
Unforgettable gifts, ornate silver platters set forth,
Directly under nostrils flared,
Worlds hovering upon geometrical surfaces,
A feast satiating emotional oceans,
Pleasing even Queen Salome Alexandra!
I did not inhale.
Pressures and pleasures profound, too profuse,
Fright beyond definition, displacing place,
Everything I wanted, only
Twenty years later; your light shines brightly,
But knowing you, your darkness also, rich and mighty!
Distill it down please, you know me best,
Look upon me and renew.

Superhuman
(For Nandini Ramakrishna)

Worth more than your tiara,
Midas touch, solid with crimson star,
Unshackle the giant cuffs weighing down both wrists,
We have bulletproof vests now!
Lasso us all, congregation of hopeful sisters,
We won't tell lies.

Bionic efforts, Herculean feats, harvest the Earth
Fulfilling others' demands, requests, needs.
You are super, it's true but
Human too . . .
You have enough hats to wear,
Outsource keys to the lair,
Quickly, as always-think fast, it is time
To run the next marathon mile,

Training, while you're at it, the next generation,
Inevitable, diaper dash nation!
Exotic Floridian palms and citrus whiffs,
Centuries aged Gothic stained glass,
Amidst alley ways of floating alligators
Adorn your tropical abode;

Park your invisible plane,
Replace your one-piece,
Your light shines more brightly
Than the red, white and blue-
Wonder Woman, it's not easy being you.

Detritus

Here it is, flotsam and jetsam of lives,
Lives loved, lived, ended, sometimes upended.
A doll with one missing button eye,
Sewed up she'll be good as new in some other crib;
A fat stone toad from someone's garden,
Now unwanted, now mere stone, scrap.
Discarded dresses, books, jewelry pieces
All garnered with relish in days gone by
Price tags fluttering in the wind, summer weaves
Rendered null and void—so much clutter, junk, or dreams—I wonder
What'll be the tag on my forehead?
Am I pushing too much,
Hoping for values where and when
They don't count, don't exist?

Signaling Dissent

I'm so upset the blood roils and the pressure
Keeps me up the whole-night—Wondering,
Didn't make myself clear, how much cruder
Can one get, asking the other to stay put.
To stay away, for now, for all eternity? Please!
Let your fingers be too stiff to punch in phone numbers,
Please, I don't want to jump for every ring,
The door, the phone, the alarm, the ear, the finger—whatever-
Did I mix metaphors, metals, against the rules
Of alchemy, facebook, all the social gobbledygook?
I say, blast all this social polite crap, the musical chairs.
How about the deliberate whittling of splinter into arrow
Dipping into deep potions, the Borgias knew about
And fusing hand and eye, just so to hit the target?
Too nuanced—let's be more direct—iron meeting dense
Iron, the clang, the clatter of hooves and dueling dust-
Alas! Gone with the medieval times-
Consider Obama with remote control-
I should drop a cluster from B52s, straight and swift,
Shrieking in the desert air, one minute; conflagration!
And then blessed silence, the rest of the night.

Cheers Felisa!

I drank what?
Socrates said.
Caught like a sneeze,
Our lives are painted *egg-shell-white*, a popular color
For hospitals,
My glass, half filled
With distilled water;
Inert, I am a veritable 'bubble-boy',
Wouldn't you know it?
Hermetic helium filled chambers . . .
Shakespeare's Puck, viewing life
While you live it,
From above, circulating, distanced,
An out of body phenomenon, are you
Human or other?

Sniffing out metabolic poisons, bloodhound, finding comfort-
Just the idea, noxious gases are
Experienced second hand through Hubble's eye,
Circulating through the Crab Nebula, Eye Of God,
Shivering involuntarily, deep space chill,
Move away, away,
Distance between us must place, things of
Such beauty, unenvisoned potential . . .

The shadow, my connected entity,
Pondering dualities,
Good and bad in proportions don't tango,
If I would but involute in circular form,
To morph Kafkaesque, into a GFAJ-1 bacterium!
My cells could feed,
Self-sustaining finally,
On the slick quicksilver of arsenic!
Defying life's boundaries, rule-breaker,
Rebel!
Good girls go to heaven,
Bad girls go
Everywhere-

This present
Requires an alternate extremophile reality.
Eking out rainbows,
Today, I will look for them
Through the rain.

Earning My Stripes

At the edge of the cliff, the view is scary.
Teetering, I take a peak—awesome scary.
But I am here I am here after all,
Through the fee-fum-fo, fiddle and fuddle,
Toil and muddle, toil and trouble,
Through the dark forest and dank swamps,
Reeking of bloody, broken teeth and gory craw;
Macheted my way up through sticky ooze,
Sucking leeches, slithering creepers and creeps,
Then, coat slimy, eyes rheumy, breath raspy,
Through the dirty white, winter wasteland, flat, void.
Up, up and away, away from all the toil and trouble!

Look, look, now my coat has lovely stripes, stark and shiny,
Russet brown on orange blending gold, black and white;
I've earned my stripes, this technicolor coat;
Can laurels be far behind?
Suddenly, someone from somewhere comes hurtling, yelling,
"Move over, déjà vu tigress, you, your colors are passé."
I'm clutching, bristles a-quiver, foot hold loosened,
One foreshortened paw; contexts change,
So do stripes and shades. I've got to go-
Once again, through Sysyphian toil and trouble,
To change my stripes, to survive!
See you later, alligator.

Leaf Fall

Sighing in the long autumn wind
A single sun mottled leaf
Dreams psychedelic enough to unwind,
Dares a take-off from tree's mothering grief.

Oh! The splendorous possibilities it signified
In its pause, shimmer, suspension and fall,
A gyrating go-between for a cause dignified,
A mystic conjuring a sign beyond recall!

Leaves fall; snakes, lizards, frogs molt
While we accumulate crusty, cursed barnacles;
'Tis hard to tell, in our human cult,
When, where soul transforms into toothed manacles.

Autumnal Lament—Asian Style

Autumn heralds tremors
Of dark, unfathomable homecoming
To old man tottering on
Slender, slippery September stilts.
The landscape is browned, rumpled,
Like an old woman's unloved skin.
Here the deep echoing gloom
From mallard green marshes
Welcomes inky brush strokes of haze
Descending in slow zither waves
From the tops of twin mountain peaks.
A sudden shock of herons
Black jade Buddhas in V formation,
Beckon to him, but he bends down
And reads in his mottled palms
The life that was,
The life that'll be.

Two Ways Of Looking At It

Fall, every wondrous year, sets ablaze, they say,
New Hampshire woods in varying striking shades
Of pink, purpled gold and rippled vermilion,
Skittery squirrels gather, they say, scattered
Nuts midst groves of scary spruce and gothic fir
And plump birds show off late plumage in lingering tangos
While the coming cold, coy maiden, plays hide and seek
Peeping around distant dun colored mountaintops.

In Manila, under a glistening melon sun,
We, brown people in tune with brown earth,
Watch the world get washed into pastels,
By rain, rain and more rain.
Cool lime green bamboo shoots sprout forth
Stream jets of sparkling water gems
On lichened rocks, lizards and one legged birds.
The shy petals of Gumamela and Kalachuchi
Fall in starry radiance, in crystal cut brilliance,
To greet the inlaid pearly iridescence
Of shower spangled autumnal days.
A dozen new sprung dreams lean out
Like baby stars cradled in dark promising rain clouds,
All part of a lived life, a loved life.

Garage Sale

Other people's junk
Are her beloved treasures:
Shells and beads,
School art works,
Colorful stubs, stamps,
Doll cut outs, shrunk dresses,
And scattered toys and parts.
There comes a spring day
She's asked to clean up-
She has seen garage sales
All around the place;
This Muppet is diligent,
Her mop with shiny brown hair-
Writes prices on post-its
And posts them all around-
Everything to go
From $1 to $20 please.
Let's keep the microwave, the oven too,
She places a $20 post-it on my lapel,
I consider it an honor-
The highest price tag on my shoulder;
But this tow headed one
Is shocked to learn
Some things sold
Cannot be reclaimed.

Who Do You Think You Are? Some Kind Of Super Star?

Yes.
The moon revolves around the earth,
The earth revolves around the sun,
I am the center of the galaxy.
Giant fiery star so bright;
King of kings-
Look upon my deeds with shock and awe . . .

On-call for me,
No sleep, no rest, but stay
Sharp! I don't suffer morons easily.
Read up, be informed, ready to discuss
World events, science, music, art, literature,
The finer things of life . . .

Do try to keep up,
Your turtle tendency forces my condescension,
Provide the stuffing, the content, the context,
Sherpa, reproductive machine,
Be all that you can be and more, all for me.
I deserve it after all I am saving the world!

I don't waste my time donning a silly red cape,
Only losers have time to ponder seascapes,
Time pass, time waste.
My multi-dimensional mind, sharper than a bullet,
Stronger than the CRAY,
My stature, taller than a skyscraper,
And such pretty face put me on a train,
To Hollywood!

It's not with ease I be me,
Why should you get to be you-
Wallowing in mediocrity?
What I can do, you must do.
What's good for me must do for you-
You appear to be higher functioning? Have
Opposable thumbs?
Do better! In everything you dither, have resolve!
But check with me first,
You know well I run the show,
You may be necessary but
Not indispensable!

Endeavor

Dirty dishes, piled mile high in the sink;
NPR belching about Libya's Barrack bombing,
Liquefaction of Fukushima, other meltdowns
Nuclear and otherwise; grime added, gradual layers of strata
Everywhere—baby in crib howling willful,
Teething; middle twins cart-wheeling atop muddied carpet,
The eldest sulking over homework, feeling victimized,
The first, the last; more she does,
More she needs to do,
Fingers itching, twitching, dreaded migraine looming, clogging
Partial visage; spring into action now!

Blaring in unison, television and radio,
All along, the fat old man
Stent stuck in heat,
Tucks fat legs under fat belly,
And calls for more beer.
Another news story, another game-
Must see T.V. mandates come first and foremost.

Scrubbing clean, soaping free,
Pots and pans, clothes and curtains, carpets and cholesterol
Standing here, few minutes long, she'd clean me too!

Coming Full Circle

Oh for the mists of autumn, up in the high hills,
Russet sunsets, speckled leaves and the nip
In the cool, clear air, as you climb up and up and up!
She sighs, climbing, bracing, baby-steps plunge one more
Steel wedge bolt into the rock face swing the rope, squeezing in
Rock pick, juggling chaos in her backpack.

Where are the hills? Out the panes, she sees this is one level plain,
Bereft,
Stretching to see to tsunami sea-
As far and wide as can be . . .
Is it the end? End of the beginning or
The other way around?
Out of time, still busy, climbing up and up,
The hills are there, in minds' muscle memory-
One bleak wintry mutilated landscape.

Hidden Hungers

There are so many hungers inside me,
Thicket of dismembered bodies, one, two . . .
Starting with the Ballerina dream at three-
Do pink tutus and silver shoes set anyone free?
Then there were the gymnasts' pathways,
Following the Olympic women, on the ramp
And out-
The tennis stars,
Basketball champs,
Swimming Thorpedos,
Academic heroes,
Marrying the one and only prince,
Life with three kids, apple pies,
And the white picket fence,
Don't forget the gingham curtains,
Blowing in the breeze;

None of these ring true,
But the dreams, the hungers continue.
Get up, push it, push the envelope they say,
But I'm happy dreaming, starving day by day.
This is not true, this is make believe, they say-
I know. Does it matter anyway?
It's all mine, my make believe, my hungry, my happy day,
I'm happy day dreaming, imagining away-
Consider me on some other planet.

Proclamations!

Come one, come all,
Lend me your ears . . .
Can you hear me?
Hear me bellowing, on this level?
Downstairs?
Only monosyllables I accept,
How well I pronounce, enunciation exact!
Wishes and whims clear,
Pick up, put down, come here!
Smiling, I keep smiling,
It makes the world wonder-
What I've been up to!

Scrunching my nose, blowing soapless bubbles,
At play, most overjoyed,
Anyone even under three, knows to work
The interactive grandparent toy;
Curls brush pink polka dots, shoulders can
Wiggle; Look what else I can do-
Shake, shake my head and
I'm not dizzy! Can you?
Hear me calling?
Wait, once more, the
Neighbors didn't catch it;
Louder, I can do!
Small in size and stature but
Being two,
Carry stout voice and fat thesaurus!

Gladiator
(For Nicole Glaes Tirrell)

Ironic statutes govern our states,
Rain on a sunny Sunday,
Don't park in fire zone,
Don't walk on wet paint-
We did it all at any rate-
Any age difference,
Didn't let that get in our way-

Cheese and cracker dinners,
Sill at work, didn't ensue,
Despite promises of pasta and tiramisu,
Automated archetypal Borg queens
And fashionistas too superior for mortal beings,
Upside down poppy skirts, standing tall-
Pull up the roots, expose the competitive maul!
Students, gal-pals, mothers and more;

Body armor pleated skirts and true grit,
Kicked up sand and sweat too thick-
The Romans had it the same way,
We do today-

Having babies at home,
Warrior women, those were
Wondrous the same as you-
Four-star generals would cringe,
Unable themselves to follow in this way,
Our numbers would unhinge,
Go instead, I with you, willing-
Where we find no path and blaze a trail!

Pep Talk

Silently tranquil nestled between
Fingers of motion, mutable skylights
Experiential through liquid filters-
Folk dancing, vermillion schools all about-
Company keeping, crimson rooted fronds-
Extant, crosshatched and prosperous;

Who could anticipate then?
A freed finger ripping asunder
Flying off, a high priced freedom;
Yearning for remaining in mothering embrace,
Happy endings are how you make them,
Advice profound, go forth make the lemonade!
Even *Nike* says, Go hard or go home-
And Xanadu's stately dome?
Built in a day? No, neither was Rome!

Blessed are the meek, for they shall
Be vice-president! In this 2011,
Re-growth should be easy breezy,
Anyone out there have Starfish abilities?
Caesar had it right in 47 B.C.-
Veni vidi vici!

Separation

Irreconcilable differences make
For a crazed state!
Silence, ceasing to communicate,
This, well known in our human cult,
We pass our time, passing ships all about–

Go our own ways if we must,
Broken by lack of longevity, grace,
Pity, wagging tongues, shaking heads, all
Cannot tourniquet, too tumultuous to face,
What to do, what to do?
How to pass the living lengths
Alone, now anew . . .

Fix this, fix it,
Too late, beat it with a stick,
Flog the dead horse,
No carrot, no worries, no worse
Off than it was before the brawling,
Should have paid heed to others' calling;

Where to habituate, self situate?
Tell the children made up stories, nonsense,
They cannot comprehend through their lens,
Pull out enormous paper work stacks, the horror
Of piles to organize for a different forever,
So much smoke,
Now there's just Fire!

Coming Full Circle

What, what did you say? Cannot do
Without you, call if off, stay?
The resolve, the determination,
Enduring, straight jawed condemnation,
What happened, the low blows were a multitude,
Fired with magnitudes of certitude . . .
Now you call for a re-initiation? A lifetime
Of wondering when's it to be just fine-
Again with repetitions and revisions . . .

Can we revisit separation? It was a kind of
Good solution!

Willow Pattern—Take I

Not to mix,
The blue and the white;
The blue on white, domineering stark and bright;
Two doves eternally murmur,
The clouds are distant but clear;
The bridge arches up and away,
The father, whip in hand, tries his usual way
Lovers, clasping tight hands, flee-
Across the meadow, past the Willow tree;
Forever will he chase the fleeting pair-
Forever wilt they be Keatsian chaste and fair.

Willow Pattern—Take II

This plantation, those colonial times,
The blue and white shard in my hands,
Unearthed, it tells stories-
Of brute times,
Sprinkled with these flowers of civility-
Of candle-lit dinners, sophisticated repartees,
August company-
Women carrying loaded platters-
Blue and white, blazing willow pattern;
Oh what jollity!
What Yankee enterprise!
Still, does anyone remember?
The soot filled kitchen,
The flaying, the flogging of indentured help?
If wishes come true
I'd love to be the bejeweled, decked out dinner guest,
Simpering politesse,
Whispering behind pomaded curls.
But what's to prevent a fateful line crossing
Becoming the carrier, the cleaner
Of the blue patterned plate,
Eaten rather than eat?
Status quo is best.

Hold The Earth
(For my favorite Sagittarian)

Didn't we . . .
Breach blood-womb barriers,
Didn't we
Follow furlongs of our hearts,
Didn't we
Dun color our positivity,
Didn't we
Prevail despite pain,
Didn't we
Fall together?
Rise up just the same?
Didn't we
Find the voices that talk up,
Can also tear down?
Didn't we
Warm the winters?
Glean through icy incantations?
Didn't we
Set down road forks and
Set upon our foes?

Shouldn't you
See how I love you,
Empty the bottles of fatigue years,
Bring back the can-do,
Beat back how they've become too few . . .

Shouldn't we
Forge forever?
Never say never?
Hold the earth?

Coming Full Circle is a culmination of twenty-five years of literary incubation. This work creates it's own ecology by drawing inspiration from within as well as from others' life experiences and the natural world. A new genre of fusion poetry, Coming Full Circle is an interactive blend of factual science and subjective fiction tossed in an existential salad-bowl for all to experience and enjoy.

Having grown up as an expatriate in Asia, Europe and North America, RKR earned several degrees in the natural sciences and literature before moving to Massachusetts to teach children, paint and write.

RUN

ENDURE THE PAIN,
KEEP THE FAITH,
FINISH YOUR RACE

FERDIE CABILING
WITH WALTER WALKER